Kabbalah:

The Tree of Life

C000064470

Meditations on the Paths to Paradise

Will Parfitt

Will Parfitt has worked in the fields of personal and spiritual development and practised Kabbalah for forty years. He trained in psychosynthesis and is a registered psychotherapist, leading courses in England and Europe. He also has a private practice in Glastonbury, England, where he lives, offering psychotherapy, mentoring, supervision and spiritual guidance.

Books by Will Parfitt

KABBALAH

The Living Qabalah
The Elements of the Qabalah
The New Living Qabalah
The Complete Guide to the Kabbalah
Kabbalah for Life

PSYCHOLOGY

Walking Through Walls
The Elements of Psychosynthesis
Psychosynthesis: The Elements and Beyond
The Something and Nothing of Death

POETRY

Through The Gates of Matter

You can find more information on Will
and his current work at his website:

www.willparfitt.com

Kabbalah:

The Tree of Life

Meditations on the Paths to Paradise

Will Parfitt

PS AVALON
Glastonbury, England

© Will Parfitt 2010

First published in the U.K. in 2010 by PS Avalon

PS Avalon
Box 1865, Glastonbury
Somerset, BA6 8YR, U.K.
www.psavalon.com

Will Parfitt asserts the moral right
to be identified as the author of this work

Design: Will Parfitt

All rights reserved. No part of this publication may be
reproduced, sorted in a retrieval system, or transmitted
in any form or by any means, electronic, mechanical,
photocopying, recording or otherwise, without the prior
permission of the publisher, except in the case of brief
quotations embodied in articles and reviews.

ISBN 978-0-9562162-1-2

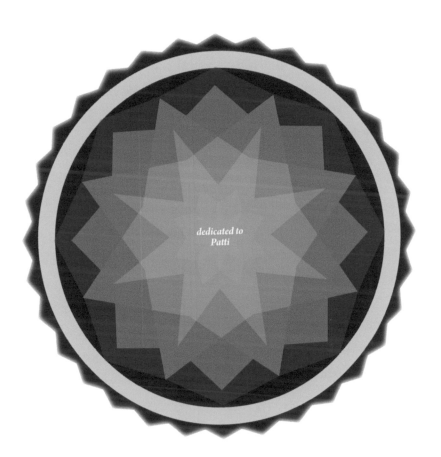

dedicated to
Patti

Introduction

She is more precious than pearls; nothing you desire can compare with her.
Her ways are pleasant ways, and all her paths are peace.
She is a Tree of Life to those who embrace her; those who lay hold of her will be blessed.

– King Solomon

The Kabbalah (alternatively spelt Qabalah or Cabala), whilst originally based on esoteric Jewish teachings, has become the heart of the Western Esoteric Tradition. A philosophy and psychology of great theoretical and practical depth, its essential message is that each individual person has the potential to realise their inner divinity and then express this in all walks of life.

In the Old Testament of the Bible there is evidence of the existence of the Kabbalah in pre-Christian times, but it was not committed to writing until the Middle Ages and much development has taken place since the Nineteenth Century.

The modern Western Kabbalah uses the Tree of Life both as a complete map of all levels of consciousness, and as a useful and potent guide to personal development. Kabbalists teach that each individual person has their own Tree of Life inside them which has to be directly experienced, not just believed in. Further, through its relevance to the evolution of the individual, it is also relevant to the evolution of the whole planet.

The Kabbalistic Tree of Life is composed of eleven spheres, representing everything from the body and the physical world through to the most central, or deepest aspect of our spiritual being, the place where our individuality blurs into union with all other consciousness. As we learn to have practical experience of these different spheres, and particularly the twenty-two paths making links between them, so we add to our knowledge of the different parts of ourselves. The Tree of Life is therefore very relevant to our modern world as a way of personal growth, interpersonal expression and spiritual connection.

There are lots of words of varying quality and worth written about Kabbalah; it is the aim of this book to offer the practitioner imagery that has the depth and connection to make the spheres and paths of the Tree of Life come to life in a non-rational, non-linear way. May the fruits of your meditation be truly more precious than pearls.

The Kabbalistic Wheel – Paths to Paradise

Anyone with ears to hear must listen to the Spirit and understand. To everyone who is victorious in this will be given fruit from the tree of life in the paradise of God.
— Revelations 2:7

Kabbalah today is an integration of practices from many different traditions and the Tree of Life imagery presented in this book is a unique and original synthesis of Kabbalistic and Medicine Wheel teachings of ancient cultures. The aim of both is to focus our attention to awaken us to our innate, inviolable and unimpeded connection to nature and natural forces, and to our relationship with the earth.

A Medicine Wheel, like the Kabbalistic Tree of Life, helps us explore our place in the universe and our relationship to all things emerging from Source. Medicine Wheel teachings stress the healing of individuals, communities and nations just as *tikkun*, reparation, is central to Kabbalah teachings. Using the Wheel enables us to understand our own lives in relation to the world in which we live, and mirrors the great wheels of our world: the cycling of seasons, the circuit of the sun, the phases of the moon.

The natural world is a continuum of consciousness; genetically we know there is very little difference between the simplest life forms and the most complex; this is true on all levels and awakening, moving beyond the confines of our limited time and space, we can embody the reality of the oneness of everything. Recognizing this oneness, that all we experience is an active emanation from the divine creative source, is the ultimate spiritual attainment. This is the paradise on earth we do not find through transcending the world, but, rather, through realising paradise is the physical world which we share with all living creatures.

When a spiritual and ecological balance is restored in the individual, then outer ecological balance is also healed. Each of us has an opportunity to reconnect with the paradise from which we haven't been banished but from which we have made a separation so that we can experience the joy of reconnection. It is my wish that the illustrations for the spheres and paths of the Tree of Life presented in this book, wisely used as reflective and meditative aids, may bring us closer to realising and embodying our oneness, and entering the living experience of paradise on earth.

A Medicine Wheel allows Kabbalistic correspondences relating to the Earth and our relationship with it to be experienced in a circular form with no beginning or end no matter which direction you travel. The Wheel is accessed through deepening connection, through intensity of experience rather than ascent or descent which are better seen as two of the six directions (with north, east, west and south).

The simplest Medicine Wheel is a cross within a circle; in Kabbalah we have two such crosses, that of the 'outer' spheres of the individual and that of the 'inner' spheres through which an individual connects to Source. The point of intersection of these two wheels is *Tiphareth*, the heart. All the other symbols, including those of the illustrations in this book, are a gradual overlaying of images intended to deepen the practitioner's understanding and increase her or his level of energy.

The centres of the 'outer' and 'inner' wheels are the access points to the great mystery of interrelatedness and connection which enable deep examination of the processes that lead us to Oneness. The 'outer' Wheel is a mirror of our inner dialogue and, through the purification of heart energy, the access point to Inner Silence. The 'inner' Wheel gathers our forces and enables communication with all levels of being, the touching of Spirit.

Meditation on the spheres ands paths of the Tree of Life gives you access to many different levels of consciousness and the illustrations in this book intend to support this process. Finding your own ways into and out of these worlds is most effective but there are a few suggestions in the notes at the back of this book to help you connect with the Kabbalistic Medicine Wheel.

Imagination and the Will – always underpinned by Love – are the main components of all mystical and esoteric systems aimed at spiritual realisation. There are many examples of using willed imagery in Kabbalah texts and even the oldest, oral methods of teaching Kabbalah through inductive story telling involve the use of powerful imagery. The images in this book offer a way of making connections using the imagination (astral) and the will (causal) to take you beyond separation and towards Oneness.

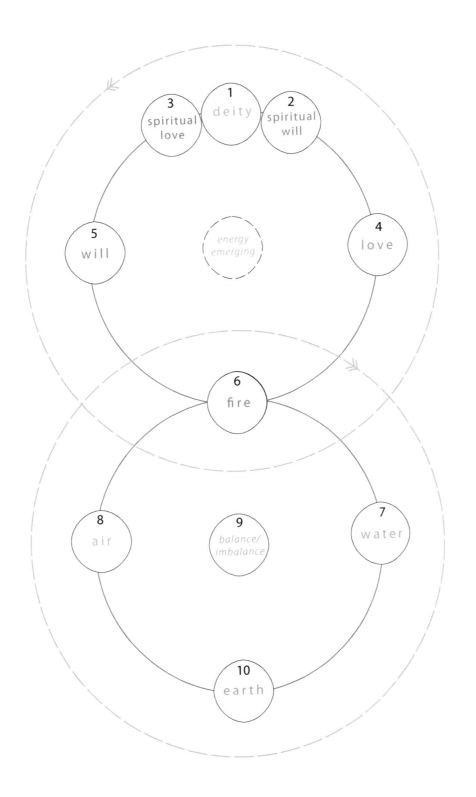

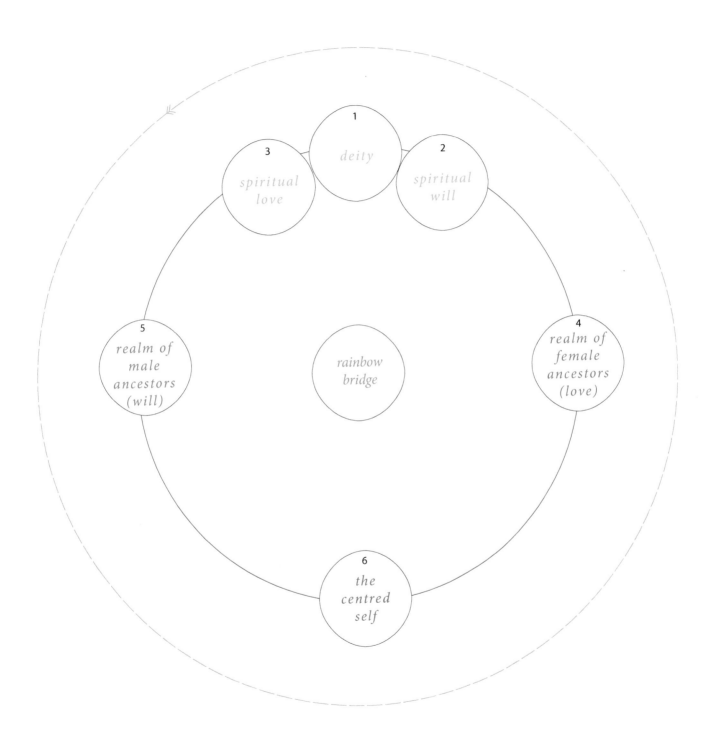

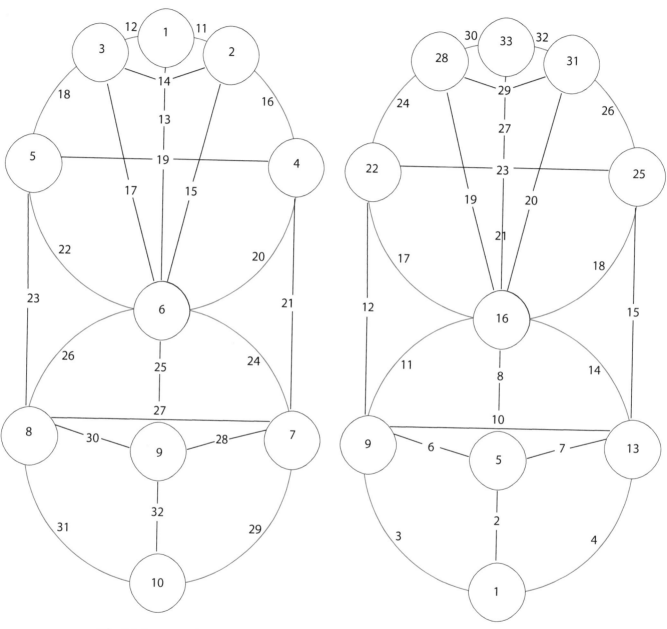

The Lightning Flash

The traditional order of the paths

on the Tree of Life

The Serpent's Path

The order of the illustrations in this book

of the paths on the Tree of Life

מלכות

Malkuth, The 10th, Sphere of the Earth

The Meadow of Delights

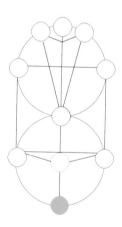

Come to this place, standing on the grass again. Today.
Here. A gate opens – there is nothing to bar the way.
When water and air and fire are balanced, earth and
spirit are united.

ת

Tau, The 32nd, Administrative Path

The Great One of the Night of Time

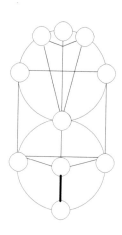

Breathe in the sweet air that crosses the water
from the temple of the secret seed. Realise all is in
wonderment, for the seed is everywhere. Gently
touch the earth.

_ש_

Shin, The 31st, Perpetual Path

The Spirit of the Primal Fire

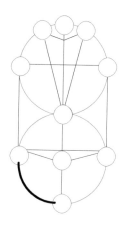

_There is a great fire ahead that is becoming the song
as it approaches the great measure of time. Be prepared
to sing the one note that the aeons recognise. Breath is
life._

Qoph, The 29th, Corporeal Path

The Entrance to the Crescent Gate

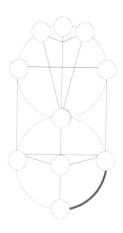

From oneness into duality and back again, the waxing and waning flow of form. There is nothing better than being still, looking at the beautiful moon. Life is not that strange, not really.

יסוד

Yesod, The 9th, Sphere of Foundation

The Secret Valley

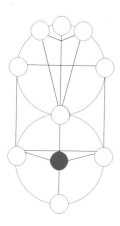

This has been experienced before, and it will be experienced again; it is always experienced now. This depth is the birth place of wisdom – until something is forgotten. There are no secrets.

ר

Resh, The 30th, Collecting Path

The Light of the World Fire

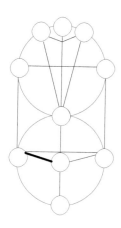

Bright light, waking dreams into nakedness.
All this is heaven; so enter this holy place. Wake here,
this time seeing. There is no moment, everything
changes.

צ

Tzaddi, The 28th, Admiral Path

The Ruler of the Depths

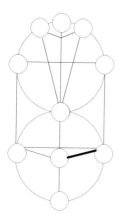

Quiet. Stop rehearsing, be here now. Stop being anyone.
Each one is seen in others. Silent words from the heart
drop to the ground.

Samekh, The 25th, Tentative Path

The Bringer Forth of Life

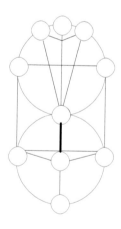

*Each world is composed of many worlds, in each world
more. Held apart and brought to One, this is the Work.
There are no other creatures on this altar. At the
moment.*

הוד

Hod, The 8th, Sphere of Thinking

The House of Spells

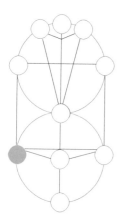

There is always perfection. Enjoy being uncertain,
that is certain. There are no enemies in this house.
This is the revelation of all teachings.

Pe, The 27th, Exciting Path

The Mouth of the Divine Fire

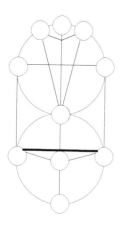

*The worlds go on irrespective of this life. Everything
changes here and now. Climb down from the midst
of unrest.*

Ayin, The 26th, Renovating Path

The Protector of the Gates of Matter

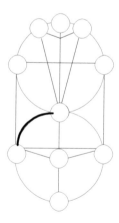

*Each body is full of the heavens. It is not where it is
going to that matters, it is where it is coming from.
No thing is negative.*

Mem, The 23rd, Stable Path

The Spirit of the Mighty Waters

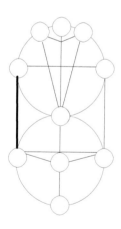

Having made it out of water, rest now. Where there is ecstasy, there is creation. The word made flesh. Things are simultaneously true and untrue.

נצח

Netzach, The 7th, Sphere of Feeling

The Garden of Beauty

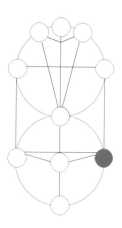

There is nothing to say when walking in beauty.
Walk the earth of this blessed place, this paradise
of abundance. Step into each now, splendour on earth.

נ

Nun, The 24th, Imaginative Path

The Entrance to the Great Renewal

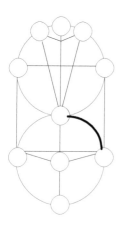

Life is but the passing of moments. There is not a day too soon nor a day too late. Die at the right time and the light door opens.

Kaph, The 21st, Conciliatory Path

The Wheel of the Forces of Fate

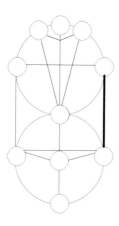

The beating of heart alone is enough to cleanse the soul.
What a blessed feeling, to be blessed. Turning the wheel
and no longer contained.

תפארת

Tiphareth, The 6th, Sphere of the Self

The Mountain of Soul

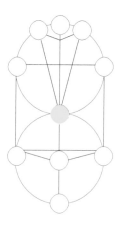

*Becoming a point at the middle of the circle, each is
beautiful in every way. This is heart, the secret seed
blending love and will, the golden realm of paradise.*

Lamed, The 22nd, Faithful Path

The Spirit of Inner Truth

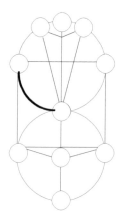

Take no action. Moving to centre, do so with caution.
Creat moments of complete silence. The mystery –
stepping inside.

ʼ

Yod, The 20th, Intelligent Path

The Seed of the Eternal

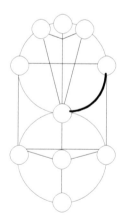

Do not strive after perfection when life is already
perfect. Allow all possibilities and the spell is broken.

Zain, The 17th, Disposing Path

The Children of Faith

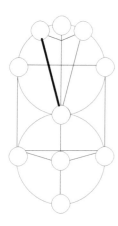

Merging, separating, one two and back again.
To look into this is to melt into bliss, one with the secret
heart. No looking for faith when faith is the source.

He, The 15th, Constituting Path

The Substance of Creation

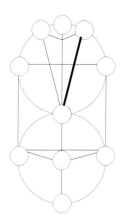

*In each of the million million worlds, at the centre
of the sphere of paradise, a window. Those connected
to wisdom, in passing, realise this permanence.*

ג

Gimel, The 13th, Uniting Path

The Priestess of the Silver Star

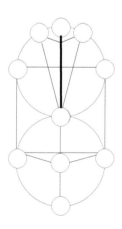

There is only one who can reach the peak. Naked
feet feel every atom of every mote on the face of this
elevated place, this mount.

גבורה

Geburah, The 5th, Sphere of Justice

The Temple of Power

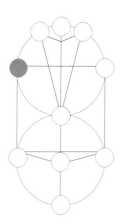

What a wondrous place this is, this earth.
Approaching the great circle of time, prepare.
Sometimes let the world evolve, sometimes stand
as a guardian of sacred places.

Teth, The 19th, Activating Path

The Children of the Dragon Flame

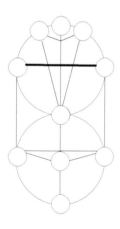

There is absolutely no longing, only belonging. The perfection of love and will, open arms, emphasizing an eternal embrace. This is a time for life. for breathing freely.

Cheth, The 18th, Influential Path

The Magus of the Light Grail

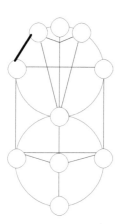

*Breath is life. A cup held to the sky then drunk long
and deep, here is the elixir. Will be done, the way this
goes, back to the start.*

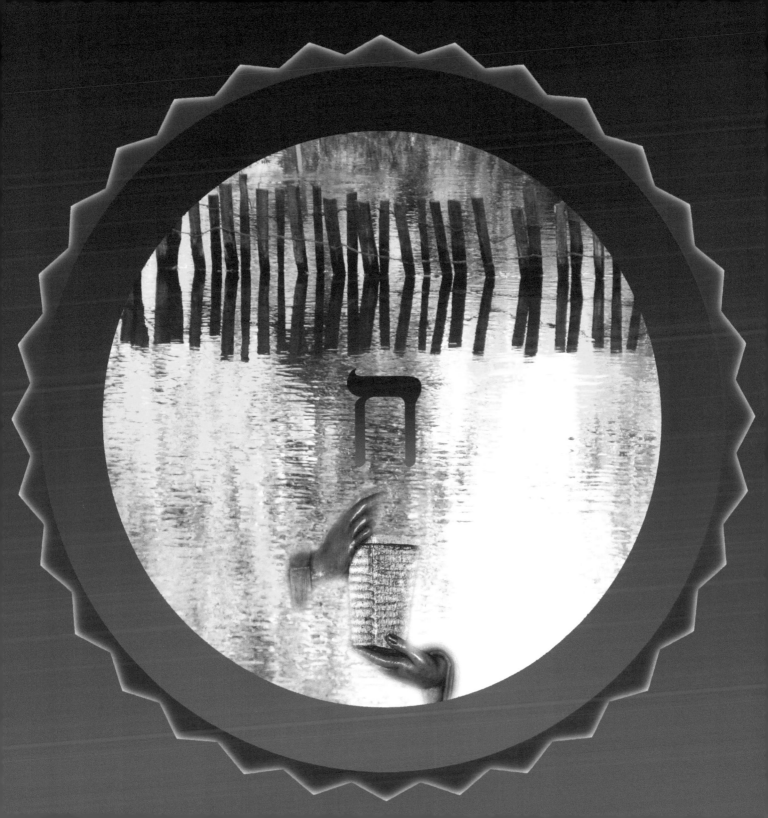

חסד

Chesed, The 4th, Sphere of Mercy

The Temple of Love

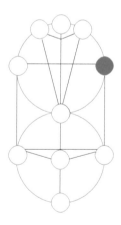

Allow what is real and not real. Blessings and curses,
they are not different. This is the most beautiful place,
the body in which Love dwells.

ו

Vau, The 16th, Eternal Path

The Magus of the Everlasting

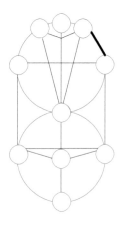

The natural priest stands tall with roots embracing
roots, a pattern of merging as natural as Love.
Each atom, embracing the air, sings silently of joy.

דעת

Daath, The Sphere that is Not

The Rainbow Bridge

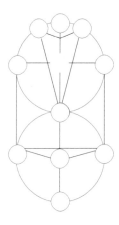

Always renewing, not having been here before, become the creator of such places. Welcome to this world.

בינה

Binah, The 3rd, Sphere of Understanding

The City of Pyramids

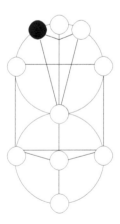

*Breathe in the sweet smelling air that pervades the holy
pyramids of secret meeting. Each one is so beautiful;
each time come here, and renew.*

ד

Daleth, The 14th, Illuminating Path

The Door of the Mighty Ones

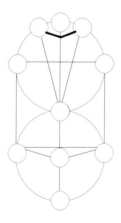

*To be without time let go into intensity. Whether this
is dreaming or being dreamed is unknown, as is real
and not real. This is nothing important.*

ב

Beth, The 12th, Transparent Path

The Spirit in the Temple

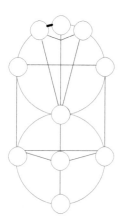

Where there is ecstasy, there is creation. Enjoy the sense
of bringing power to earth, empowering the land; walk
silently, alone. Born out of the world at each moment.

חכמה

Chockmah, The 2nd, Sphere of Wisdom

The Crown of Creation

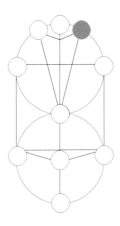

Cosmic creation is always mystery, a wonderful mystery.
Walk in this world with the silence of rabbit, the stealth
of cat, the humour of human.

א

Aleph, The 11th, Scintillating Path

The Spirit of the Aethyrs

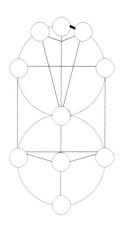

Stepping lightly down the spiral, bless every thing.
Welcome encounters with the beauty of nature – the
light, the trees, the sky, there is no difference. Life is.

כתר

Kether, The 1st, Sphere of Spirit

The Innermost Temple

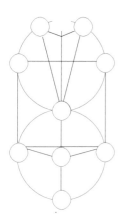

Each body is beautiful, smells sweetly and is full
of great laughter. Take a deep breath and the air is
pure, the earth, innermost spirit energized.
Enter paradise, here today.

Suggestions for exploring the Tree of Life Illustrations

The practices that follow offer you experiential ways to connect with the Kabbalistic illustrations in this book. Before starting any of the activities, ensure you have enough time without being disturbed. Be aware that you are a unique individual being choosing at this unique time to perform this activity.

It is a good idea to keep a record of your work with the Tree of Life in a journal as, apart from anything else, it helps you to ground your experience and find ways of expressing what you have learned in your everyday life. Also remember that taking a light approach can help you connect with the work and keep a perspective on it.

Still yourself before all Kabbalistic activities, using the *Kabbalistic Cross* to focus and align yourself with the Tree of Life. After all activities, ground yourself back into your physical body and your everyday world.

The Kabbalistic Cross

The Kabbalistic Cross is useful because it connects us with the Tree of Life through our physical form; it aligns energies and balances our auras; and it acts as a barrier or protection device to stop unwanted intrusions into our space. Following the instructions below, the Kabbalistic Cross need only take a few moments once you are familiar with it. Re-read this even if you already know other versions of the Cross. Note well not to rush such work – be clear with each stage before moving onto the next. It is better to go too slowly than to go too fast.

Relax and centre yourself. Stand upright, attentive but not stiff. Pronounce each word slowly and with much resonance.

Touch your forehead with the forefinger of your right hand and say: **ateh** ('for thine') – be aware of your deepest inner connection. [You might prefer to say 'for mine' aligning with Source and removing the temporal distinction between 'thine' and 'mine']

Move your finger down in a straight line to touch your lower belly area and say: **malkuth** ('is the kingdom' [or 'is the earth']). – be aware of your whole body.

[You might like to add in 'adonai' – 'my lord' in English – as you pass and lightly touch the area in the middle of your chest.]

As you mover your finger as instructed, visualise each line drawn on your body as shining, silver-white light, which permeates your astral, etheric and physical bodies.

Bring your finger straight back up to your chest then move it across to the right.

Touch your right shoulder, and say: **ve geburah** ('the power' [or 'the courage']) – be aware of your power.

Drawing a line across to touch your left shoulder, say: **ve gedulah** ('and the glory' [or 'the compassion']) – be aware of your love energy.

Clasping your hands together over your heart, visualise a shining white cross inscribed over your body.

Say: **le olahm** ('unto the ages') – be aware of exactly where you are (here), exactly at this moment (now).

Extend your arms out so you are standing as a cross, and say: **amen**

Stay standing for a while, feeling the energy to which you've connected permeating your physical and psychic space.

The Lightning Flash

After centering yourself, picture the Tree of Life as overlaying your body. Imagine a bolt of lightning manifests from nothingness and enters the top of your head at Kether. From there, without any deviation, it travels through the remaining spheres (that is, to Chockmah on the left side of your head, to Binah on the right side of your head, Chesed left shoulder, Geburah right shoulder, Tiphareth at heart, Netzach at left belly and hip, Hod at right belly and hip, Yesod at genitals level, Malkuth at your feet.)

As you visualize this, make the energy flow continuous, not so much a flash as a streaming of light. The energy pauses at each sphere to charge it up and to vitalize its essence. Then the energy flows on until it arrives at Malkuth. You can now feel the Tree complete, all the spheres lit with bright lights. Realise yourself as connected to Malkuth and channel this continuously flowing energy into Malkuth as now flowing into you. Accept this energy and take it into yourself. Allow it to fill you in whatever way feels right for you.

The Ascending Serpent

After the primary ten lights were illuminated by the lightning flash, lesser lights sprang up between them, to become the paths. The spheres can be reached through taking on the form of a serpent which is the archetypal model for climbing the paths. By twisting and turning focus about on the Tree, a human mind can both reach the heights of spirit and choose to return to matter.

Be open to receive – a vital activity! Being receptive to the energies of different illustrations as you deepen your connection to the Tree of Life requires you to do invocation: after centering yourself, call down the energy of the sphere or path being explored, right into your realm.

Entering Inner Silence

Relax and centre yourself. Now let go of your everyday inner dialogue and let your attention focus instead on your breathing, not changing it in any way, but just its natural rhythm.

Allow *Inner Silence* to be in your body, and assume a posture that expresses this quality. Relax your tensions, let them drift away. Breathe slowly. Allow *Inner Silence* to express itself on your face. Visualize yourself with that expression.

Invoke the quality of *Inner Silence*. Imagine you are in a place where you feel *Inner Silence*; a quiet beach, in a Temple of *Inner Silence*, wherever you choose. Try to really feel it. Let the quality of *Inner Silence* permeate you, to the point of identification if possible. Allow yourself to be *Inner Silence*.

Focus on the image of the path you are exploring… trust what comes and allow it to develop, to change, to become stronger, whatever the imagery does… look at it closely, consider its colour, depth, light, any specific features of this image.

Now gently bring yourself back to your everyday consciousness and do something to ground your energy.

The Circle of Connection

Create a clear circle in which to work. Your circle will enable you to define the boundaries for your work. It will also, in the case of this ritual, act as a container for your invocation of energies from the spheres and paths on the Tree of Life. Find the centre of your circle, then stand quietly whilst sensing the outer boundaries of the circle.

State your intention: to explore your chosen illustration. Do something to connect with the earth, for instance, stamp your feet, touch the ground in all directions, and so on.

Do some vigorous activity (movement, dance *or any other activity* that shifts you from your usual, everyday state of awareness and raises your energy.) Start gently then keep at it until you feel you cannot do any more. Then continue for at least another minute or two.

Standing at the centre of your circle facing north, gather all your forces and energies. Place your illustration at the centre *then step out of the circle, turn around and face back into it.*

Project into the circle your desire to connect with the sphere or path represented by this imagery. When ready, step into the circle, pick up the illustration and holding it before you, connect to this energy within yourself.

When you feel ready, close the circle by standing at the centre, feeling stillness pervading you, then stamp your feet, affirming your intention to fully close your circle.

Behind The Curtain

Sitting or lying comfortably with a dim light in your room (candle light is ideal), close your eyes and breathe deeply.

Imagine the image has been painted clearly and brightly on a fine, almost invisible curtain. For now do not go past the curtain but imagine you look beyond to see what is behind it. Allow the emerging images to appear before you. Do not judge or censor them.

If it feels right for you, you may go through the curtain and step into the world you see there. If you decide to do this, only go a little way into this world. You can always return at another time if you wish.

Whether you go into the world behind the curtain or not, when you have finished firmly and willfully close the curtain and purposely step out of the world being explored.

Lighting the Spheres

Imagine a bright white light hovering over your head then draw this white light down into your heart where it glows like a bright yellow sun. This yellow light fills up all the space around you, pervading all directions with bright yellow light.

Imagine white light above your head again. visualising it flowing down into your yellow heart, then feel this light flow down into your lower body, your genital area, your legs, into and around your feet. A clear and bright purple energy pervades your lower body, connecting you to the ground beneath you. Then feel the presence of your feet on the floor, fully supported by the earth.

Keep the sense of the white light flowing down from above you, down through your glowing yellow heart, down into a purple light where you are in contact with the ground. Imagine you are surrounded by a deep and intense blue aura surrounding and protecting you.

Affirm this blue light brings you fully into manifestation, so that all that you are is here right now.

Again feel the presence of the white light above your head, down through your glowing yellow heart, down to the purple light in your lower body and where you contact the ground. Be aware of the blue aura surrounding you.

Now focus on your chosen illustration and allow the energies it represents to enter your orbit. Keep drawing the energy in until you feel full. Stay with this for as long as you sense is appropriate, then very carefully bring yourself back to your physical, everyday world and do something mundane to fully ground yourself back to earth.

Notes

First Principle.

Do unto others as you would have them do unto you. This is the ground of Kabbalah, that love underpins all else; the 'secret' is to add 'will' to 'love' – to direct love, and then let it go.

Energy Bodies.

The *etheric body* is closely associated with the 'physical body' (etheric is the 'energy field' of the physical form) (Malkuth).

The *astral body* is associated with the emotional realm; emotions are not 'astral' but just as the physical creates an etheric double or energy field, so the emotional life creates an astral double or energy field (Yesod).

The *mental body* (the 'causal' body) is associated with 'rational functions' i.e. thoughts and feelings (the plane of Netzach and Hod).

The *spiritual body* is an energy field corresponding to (or 'created by') deeper soul connections or the finer energy within us (the middle triangle).

The etheric body is located very close to the physical (a centimetre or so away); the astral extends outwards (in a resting healthy body to about an arm's length); the mental body extends beyond that with a diffuse outer edge that blends into its surroundings which are then created in form through the operation of this body; the spiritual body doesn't exist in this time/space continuum. These distances vary, for instance: the etheric can sink to the level of the feet, a remnant of its former glory; the astral body expands/contracts continually, depending upon energy level, physical and emotional health; the mental body sometimes becomes so enmeshed in the outside world it is indistinguishable from its surroundings; sometimes even the spiritual body can recede and virtually disappear.

Colours.

With true psychic vision there is no right or wrong; we see energy then overlay colour onto it, and different psychics overlay different colours. Certainly the 'usual' book version with chakras (that is, using the spectrum colours upwards, red for base chakra through to violet for crown chakra) is very neat and clever but no psychic really sees these colours which are astral fantasies.

With the Tree of Life, anyone can use their own colours, but the advantage of using the colours we use is that they are not psychic, astral/etheric colour schemes (which change with the viewer) but are archetypal patterns of colour that are the deepest connection to colour and energy that can be described.

Physical Locations.

There are special places in the body that each person has to locate and pinpoint accurately for themselves. Where paths cross, locate these power places in the body; for instance, 1-6 crosses 4-5 in the well of the neck where the shoulder bones meet.

For locations within the Supernal Triangle, particularly significant is where 1-6 crosses 2-3 in the centre of the head, manifesting physically in the 'third eye'. Through physical/energetic manipulation of this centre we are able to increase/decrease psychic awareness.

It is generally unwise to let another being (of any kind) touch these special places. As for you, try stroking and lightly feathering the place and feel the energy spread.

Using both tension and relaxation at the same time, tense in a relaxed way, relax in a tensed way. Tension is holding your intent in a relaxed way, without lust after result. Then the energies permeate lower spheres and bring effects.

Lightning Source UK Ltd.
Milton Keynes UK
UKHW050612171122
412329UK00002B/30